Original title:
The Pomegranate's Secrets

Copyright © 2025 Creative Arts Management OÜ
All rights reserved.

Author: Oliver Bennett
ISBN HARDBACK: 978-1-80586-238-3
ISBN PAPERBACK: 978-1-80586-710-4

Unraveling the Grains of Time

In a fruit so bright, with secrets to chase,
You'll find a mystery, a colorful face.
Each seed is a joke, a playful surprise,
Pop one in your mouth and watch it rise!

The juice starts to tickle, a burst of delight,
A giggle escapes, it's quite the sight.
Sipping the nectar, oh what a treat,
It's like running a race with candy conceits!

Grandma once claimed, they're tiny little spies,
Reporting your secrets to friends in the skies.
But really, they're just a mischievous crew,
Laughing and dancing, saying, "What'll you do?"

So grab them in handfuls and share with a cheer,
Tell stories of fruit that brings laughter near.
With every red gem, a giggly surprise,
Unravel the fun, let your laughter rise!

Beneath the Crimson Dome

A fruit so bright, it glows like fire,
With ruby seeds, they never tire.
But when you crack that shiny shell,
Inside lies chaos, oh what the hell!

Juicy gems that bounce and roll,
Perfect for munching, but where's the hole?
They jump around like they're in a race,
It's like a circus in that funny space!

Tides of Bitter and Sweet

Biting in, it's sweet surprise,
But one wrong chew, it's like a lie.
The taste is mixed, a playful jest,
A fruit that teases, never rests.

Sipping juice like it's a game,
You laugh and curse, who is to blame?
With every bite, you'll dance and squeal,
This fruity trap is a comic meal!

Layers of Granate

Peeling back layers, what do you find?
A mess of seeds, all intertwined.
They giggle and squirm when you take a bite,
It's a juicy riot, oh what a sight!

Each little jewel, a poppin' surprise,
Who knew they'd dance right before your eyes?
It's a party trick, this fruity delight,
A crunchy laugh in the daylight!

Veiled Truths in the Grove

In the orchard, a mystery waits,
A fruity riddle, the laughter creates.
Under leaves, a hidden spree,
What's inside? It's fun, oh me!

Seeds are plotting their joyous escape,
With every pop, they twist and reshape.
A comedic burst, an unexpected treat,
This silly fruit can't be beat!

Eden's Forbidden Offering

In the garden, lush and bright,
A fruit hung out of sight.
Eve had plans to take a bite,
But Adam said, "That's not polite!"

A serpent whispered, oh so sly,
"Just one taste, you'll learn to fly!"
But later he would simply sigh,
When fruit stains made his trousers die.

The Fruit of Knowledge and Regret

He took a nibble, juicy red,
With every bite, his fears he fed.
Now headaches dance inside his head,
Regrets, oh boy, where's my bed?

"But I'm so smart!" he told the snake,
Its laughter made his wisdom shake.
The prize was lost for wisdom's sake,
Now he just hopes for autumn's cake.

Hushed Conversations in Scarlet Flesh

In whispers soft, the fruit did speak,
A tale of daring, bold and cheek.
"We juicy jewels can make you weak,
But really, can you handle peak?"

The seeds giggled, sneaky and sly,
While birds overhead just flew by.
With every crunch, they'd laugh and sigh,
"The truth be told, you'll never fly!"

Beneath the Ruby Veil

Underneath a veil so fine,
Secrets dance like frothy wine.
If you peek too close, you might find,
A sticky truth that's quite divine.

In laughter shared, the whispers grew,
A harvest feast for just a few.
They'll tell you tales that seem so new,
But friendship's bond, that's what they brew!

Roots Tied to Ancient Mythos

In a garden where legends bloom,
Fruits giggle, dispelling gloom.
With every bite, a tale takes flight,
As humor sprouts in the soft moonlight.

Fables dance upon each skin,
While squirrels conspire to sneak a grin.
Ancient wisdom, ripe and spry,
Leaves us wondering, oh my my!

Enchanted Orchard of Longing

In an orchard where wishes grow,
Fruitful laughter on every row.
Squirrels wearing hats, quite absurd,
Chattering secrets softly heard.

Trees gossip with flickering leaves,
As bees buzz by with tales that weave.
A giggling breeze, so light and bright,
Makes longing feel a pure delight.

Crimson Seeds of Mystery

Crimson seeds underneath the shade,
Play hide and seek, the ambush laid.
With every crunch, a chuckle flows,
Unraveling jest where laughter grows.

Tiny whispers in each bite,
Relics of joy that take their flight.
Mysteries nested, soft as dew,
Tickling our minds with joy anew.

Veils of Juicy Whispers

Veils hang low, juicy and sweet,
Promises of giggles in every treat.
A fruit so bold, with tales so sly,
Whispers of hilarity flutter by.

Nature's jesters in vibrant hue,
Crafting laughter from morning dew.
Sips of joy, from nectar's seam,
Life's absurdities, a fruit-filled dream.

Tales from a Mahogany Grove

In a grove where trees wear crowns,
Squirrels gossip about the towns.
They giggle at the fruits so round,
Wonder what secrets can be found.

One day a bird flew past with flair,
With tales of fruits that dance in air.
The trees did sway, the branches swung,
And laughter from the leaves was flung.

A bear in shades came for a snack,
But tripped and fell, went off the track.
The critters laughed, oh what a sight,
As he got up, still holding tight.

And in that grove, beneath the boughs,
Life's silly moments earn the bows.
Every fruit knows, with each delight,
Nature laughs away at every bite.

Enigmas of the Lush Labyrinth

In a maze of greens where laughter blooms,
A chicken plotted, yoked in glooms.
She chased her tail, found a red sphere,
Claimed it held whispers only dear.

A rabbit popped out, quite perplexed,
"Don't eat it! That fruit's a hex!"
But the chicken chuckled, gobbled away,
While the rabbit fretted, 'This isn't my day!'

The walls of green began to twist,
As a mouse sang tunes, none could resist.
"Join me, dear friends, in merry jest,
For secrets are best when shared in fest!"

And so they danced, with hops and spins,
In the labyrinth where silliness wins.
Every secret shared with a giggle or two,
Turns the maze into a grand hullabaloo!

Beneath the Rind: A Heartbeat

In a patch where jellybeans grow,
Lived a heart who wanted to show.
It bounced around, it rolled with glee,
Squeezed in jest, "Come jump with me!"

A ticklish vine wore glasses askew,
And shouted, "Hey, what's wrong with you?
You giggle and jiggle with no fright,
Let's paint the world in colors bright!"

They tossed around seeds, what a delight,
A fat bee buzzed, "This feels just right!"
But he stumbled, slipped, and fell in a patch,
Surrounded by laughter, what a catch!

And every beat beneath that rind,
Held a rhythm only fun could find.
Their joy spread wide like sunlit rays,
In the heart of nature, where laughter stays.

Cursed Blessings of Nature's Craft

In a garden where shadows play tricks,
Whispers of fruits and a hidden mix.
A snail named Bob claimed he was wise,
With tales of fruits, oh what a prize!

"Beware the red ones, they talk at night,
Trade secrets for luck—what a fright!"
A gopher chuckled, peeking from dirt,
"More like they yell when stepped on—Ouch, it hurts!"

The flowers swayed, with petals of mirth,
As butterflies swirled, spreading their girth.
"Join us!" they cheered, in a fanciful frock,
"To taste joy in every mystery's clock!"

And so they pranced, with giggles and glee,
In a world where whimsy was all you could see.
Cursed or blessed, who cares, let's play,
For nature's crafts are a feast every day!

The Taste of Ancestral Yearnings

From ancient trees, with boughs that sway,
Juicy gems make all hearts play.
A bite brings laughter, oh so sweet,
As sticky fingers dance with glee.

Granules burst, in cheeks they hide,
Like little treasures, oh what a ride!
An heirloom snack, from days of yore,
With every munch, we crave for more.

Secrets Wrapped in Silken Skin

A shiny orb, so bold, so red,
Hides giggles and whispers, just like bread.
Peel it back, what a sight to see,
Spritz of juice, like a fruit party spree!

Each aril pops with a playful cheer,
Who knew the fun was so near?
In each little jewel, a joke does dwell,
A burst of laughter, can't you tell?

A Dance of Fragile Spheres

In bowls they roll, these round ballet stars,
Twirling around like tiny blue cars.
A sip of juice, a splash of mirth,
As sticky laughs adorn the earth.

Whirl in delight, a juicy fiesta,
Needs no DJ, just pop the vespa!
Take a bite, oh what a crunch,
Every nibble, a giggly punch!

The Last Drop of Sweetness

As the day wanes, with joy we bask,
It's time for a taste, if we dare to ask.
One last drop of that ruby bliss,
A fruity kiss, none should miss!

Like nectarous giggles, it drips slow,
A giggle here, a laugh with a glow.
Savor the sweetness, let's not waste,
For with every drop, joy's perfectly placed!

Elixir of the Sun

In the grove where the sun does play,
Fruits giggle as they plan their day.
A silly fruit with a crown so bright,
Claims it's the best, oh what a sight!

Juicy jokes spill from bursting skin,
Beneath the laughter, secrets spin.
A sip of cheer in every bite,
Making dull moments feel just right.

With each red seed, a punchline's passed,
Quips and jests that are built to last.
Who knew fruit could bring such mirth?
Unveiling joy and endless worth!

So take my hand, let's dance around,
In the orchard where smiles abound.
A sunny elixir of merry spree,
Come taste the fun, just you and me!

The Bursting Truths

Red globes laugh, it's no surprise,
With each twist, more fun complies.
They burst with giggles, oh what a mess,
Spilling secrets in wild excess.

When I bite down, it's a juicy riot,
The truths fly out, we can't deny it.
Seeds scatter like confetti bold,
Unraveling tales that are pure gold.

The skin may claim to hold it tight,
But giggling kernels take to flight.
In this fruit, tricks are bound to flow,
An orchard of laughter put on a show!

So gather round, let's share the roar,
With every bite, we'll laugh some more.
Bursting truths with every crunch,
Join the revel, it's a fruity brunch!

A Dance of Scarlet Kernels

Amidst the leaves, a bouncy beat,
Scarlet kernels tap their feet.
Round and round in jolly lines,
They swirl as if they've crossed some vines.

With each shake, a chuckle's heard,
Dancing fruits form quite the herd.
A jig of joy, a burst, a spin,
In a fruity dance, we all join in!

As seeds collide in vibrant grace,
They wink and grin with every trace.
What a party on this lively stage,
Red delights running wild and sage.

So take my hand, let's twirl away,
In this fruity fun, we'll dance and sway.
With laughter ringing, loud and bright,
Our fruity gala lasts all night!

Whispering Hues of Desire

In the garden where colors play,
Whispers float on a breezy day.
Red tongues wag with secrets sweet,
Chasing dreams on their tiny feet.

Desire drips from juicy grin,
As seeds spill tales of where they've been.
With every taste, mischief reigns,
A flood of laughs in sweet terrains.

Crimson wishes, bold and spry,
Each kernel holds a cheeky sigh.
Unwrap the joy, let the stories flow,
In this cheeky dance, let's steal the show!

So pluck a fruit, take a bite,
Join the fun, it feels so right.
In whispers soft, oh what a tease,
Laughter blooms with every squeeze!

The Weight of Hidden Riches

Beneath the skin, a treasure lies,
Rich gems that wait, a sweet surprise.
Crimson orbs with tales to share,
A fruit so bold, it dares to care.

It sits so proud upon the shelf,
A fruit with secrets of its self.
Who knew such wealth could hide in red?
These juicy jewels fill hearts with dread.

I took a bite, my taste buds danced,
With every crunch, my tongue enhanced.
But oh the seeds, they fought me back,
A messy battle—a juicy snack!

So here I sit, a sticky plight,
With juice that glows, a comical sight.
Who knew such wealth could spark a grin?
A fruit of laughter, where fun begins!

Beneath the Surface: Unveiling Heritage

A knock-knock joke from generations past,
Each layer hides tales, colorful and vast.
Peel me back, oh take a look,
Life's a recipe, a funny book.

Each seed a story, packed so tight,
Like family gatherings, oh what a sight!
Grandma's wisdom, a quirky quirk,
Unraveling secrets with each little perk.

Beneath the surface, laughter thrives,
In home-cooked meals where joy survives.
The joy of spills, the giggles of glee,
Who knew a fruit could set us free?

So let's embrace this fruity jest,
With sweetness in hand, we'll all invest.
In every bite, a laugh we'll find,
The juiciness of life, hilariously kind!

Echoes of Generations Amidst the Seeds

In every seed, an echo rings,
Chasing the laughter that heritage brings.
Like a comedy show from long ago,
Each bite a punchline, a fruit-themed show.

Splat! The juice flies across the room,
A fruity fountain—a burst of bloom.
Grandpa's jokes, oh how they land,
Juicy humor from a sticky hand.

Generations drawn to gather 'round,
With tales of old, where giggles abound.
Seeds of wisdom, seeds of fun,
The laughter's golden, the joy's well-spun.

So let's raise a cheer, let's toast to this,
A fruit that offers more than bliss.
With every crunch, we shall reprise,
The echoes of laughter, our fun-filled prize!

The Tango of Juicy Whispers

In the orchard where mischief grows,
Fruits in frolic, as the wind blows.
A tango of whispers, so sweetly absurd,
These juicy fruits spread the funniest word.

They shimmy and shake, with a playful wink,
Each burst of flavor makes us think.
Who knew such fruit could dance so wild?
A cheeky giggle from nature's child.

A splash of juice, a burst of fun,
Like stories spun 'round the evening sun.
From wobbly bites and pops that clink,
To laughter shared over a clumsy drink.

So join the dance, don't miss the show,
With every seed, let laughter grow.
In the salsa of sweetness, we find delight,
Tango with joy, from morning till night!

Revelations of the Sundrenched Skin

In the orchard under the sun,
Giggling fruits, oh what fun!
Juicy squishes, poppin' delight,
Seeds fly out, a silly sight!

With each bite, a juice cascade,
Sticky fingers, kids parade.
Nature's jester, bursting bright,
Who knew snacks could take flight?

In the shade, a juicy feast,
Nature's laughter, joy released.
Bouncing seeds, like tiny darts,
Tell me now, where do they start?

Oh, the taste of sun and cheer,
A fruity film, nothing severe.
Underneath the skin so bold,
Hidden giggles, stories told!

Unveiling Nature's Puzzle

A riddle wrapped in ruby red,
Bursting forth, just like it said.
Squeeze it tight, hear the pop,
Laughter flows, and won't just stop!

Seeds like jewels, tucked inside,
Nature's surprise, it's like a ride.
With playful seeds to toss and play,
Who knew snacks could cause a fray?

In the garden, secrets grow,
Whispers exchanged, a funny show.
Juicy bites and playful tricks,
Nature's whimsy, full of quirks!

Pull the peel, oh what a thrill,
Silly faces, laughter will spill.
Unlock the magic, twist and twirl,
With each taste, a goofy whirl!

Flavor of the Forgotten

A little fruit, once left behind,
Beneath the leaves, a treasure find.
Open wide, the flavors play,
Funny faces in disarray!

Unwrapping smiles, what a treat,
Each burst of juice, a dance, oh fleet.
Tickled tastebuds, laughter brims,
Sip the joy, whimsy swims!

Memories of summers past,
Who knew a fruit could be such a blast?
With every bite, a story told,
Of silly antics, brave and bold.

Rediscovered, vibrant and sweet,
Taking you back to childhood's beat.
Flavorful bursts and giggles pop,
In this orchard, smiles won't stop!

Beneath the Outer Layer

Peeling back the layers bright,
What's hiding here? A silly sight!
Juicy treasures, ruby bright,
Nature's joke, pure delight!

With each layer, giggles rise,
Who knew fruit could be such a surprise?
Sneaky seeds, oh, what a game,
Each slice reveals a burst of fame!

In the field, it's a playful scene,
Messy hands, joy in between.
Underneath their red disguise,
Laughter echoes, bright and wise.

So take a bite, and don't you fear,
Nature's puzzle brings us cheer.
With a wink and fruity tease,
So much fun, like buzzing bees!

Intricate Patterns of Desire

In the garden, colors spin,
A fruit so bright, where to begin?
With seeds like jewels, oh what a treat,
I wonder if they're tasty or bittersweet.

Peeling back layers, oh what a chore!
Squishing my fingers, juice galore!
I lick my palms, high hopes in tow,
Now I'm just sticky, yet craving more.

Glistening pearls, they dance around,
In every bite, sweet chaos found.
Not a fruit, but a treasure chest,
Full of giggles, and a messy quest.

So here's to feasting with glee today,
In a pomegranate world, we lose our way.
With every bite, a burst of cheer,
Who knew this fruit could be so dear?

Secrets in Each Bite

Beneath the skin, a riddle lies,
A juicy puzzle in disguise.
With every crunch, a pop, a shout,
What's this fruit really about?

Crown of red, like royalty's head,
But sticky fingers fill with dread.
I unearth treasures, seeds that sing,
What's inside? Oh! A grape? A king?

Each bite's a mystery, such delight,
Like a comedy show, tastes take flight.
Falling down, laughter is a must,
Fruit salad chaos, it's a fun bust.

I'll share with friends, let them explore,
This fruit of secrets leaves us wanting more.
In messy joys, we find our fate,
Pomegranate puzzles, oh isn't life great?

The Burst of Life

In a bowl of wonder, I take my stand,
This bouncy fruit, oh isn't it grand?
With bursts of flavor, a laugh or two,
Who knew fruit could act so askew?

Tapping on skins, I'm trying to pry,
Studying their shapes, oh me, oh my!
Juice drips down like a toddler's art,
It's both a challenge and a tart start.

With every chomp, I'm taken aback,
Seeds flying free, it's a juicy attack!
My friends all laugh at the mess we make,
Our giggles echo, as giggles do quake.

So here we are, in fruity delight,
A burst of life under the moonlight.
Each splash of red brings joyful screams,
In this fantastic, fruit-filled dream!

Threads of Ruby and Gold

Threads of ruby tangled with fate,
In this fruit, life's odd, yet great.
Peeling back dreams with every twist,
Oh, look! A gem that I can't resist!

Rows of jewels like a fairy tale,
This fruit must surely have a trail.
Juicy secrets all prone to spill,
If laughter's a crime, then I'll fit the bill.

Each tiny nugget, a tale to tell,
In sweeted insanity, I find my spell.
My hands are a canvas, red as a rose,
With every bite, my hee-haw grows.

So gather round for the fruity spree,
Join the muddled fun, you'll see what I see.
In ruby and gold, let laughter take hold,
This fruit of wonders is worth its weight in gold!

Exquisite Riddles Bursting Forth

In the garden, laughter swells,
With fruits that tell their tales.
A whisper here, a giggle there,
Who knew they had such vivid gales?

Round and ruby, a cheeky tease,
Packed with tales of summer breeze.
Pop one open, and here you'll find,
A heart that's playful, never at ease.

Juicy jewels in a sneaky waltz,
Twirling stories, causing somersaults.
Taste the chaos, it's quite absurd,
Each seed a laugh, or a gossip swirls.

With every bite, a giggle sprouts,
Who knew sweet bites came with doubts?
In this banquet of tangled cheer,
Delight awaits where folly routes.

An Offering of Juicy Secrets

Beneath the leaves, the whispers grow,
Chattering seeds in a crimson show.
Sip the laughter, taste the fun,
An offering for everyone!

Sticky fingers and cheeky grins,
As bright as the laughter that quietly spins.
Glimpse the shadows, hear the sighs,
Every bite holds a sweet surprise.

Grappling giggles with every crunch,
Beneath the surface, there's a bunch!
Who would think a fruit could play,
Comedy central, all day!

Seeds of humor, bursting bright,
In a tiny world, taking flight.
With each explosion, joy unfolds,
In a fruit so sly, its secrets told.

Blooming Shadows of a Hidden Fruit

Under leaf and bough, they tease,
With cheeky grins and buzzing bees.
Secrets twinkle, ripe and round,
In shadows where the giggles abound.

Crimson wonders, woven tight,
Peeking through the leaves, what a sight!
One bite pulls laughter from within,
The dance of shadows begins to spin.

With every slice, a story springs,
Of silly wrestles and comic flings.
Forget your troubles, drop your frown,
For here in layers, joy wears a crown.

Even hidden, they can't contain,
The joyous laughter from the strain.
In every blush, a tale to share,
Blooming shadows, secret flair.

The Garden's Untold Stories

In the garden where laughter grows,
Untold tales, a secret prose.
With every munch, and every gleam,
There's humor hidden in the cream.

Nutty giggles beneath the skin,
A riddle wrapped, where dreams begin.
What colors hide in playful jest?
Each slice may leave you quite impressed.

Seeds of wit in every bite,
Will spring forth laughter, pure delight.
Join the feast, embrace the cheer,
In the garden, secrets draw near.

Charming whispers in breezy air,
Sweet surprises in joyful glare.
A tale of folly, bright and spry,
In the garden where stories lie.

Jewel of the Orchard

In the orchard bright and fair,
A jewel hides without a care.
With laughter bouncing 'round its skin,
Who knew such fun could dwell within?

A burst of juice, a hint of tease,
Makes every bite a messy breeze.
With ruby seeds that dance and sway,
It's fruit confetti every day!

So come and take a tasty chance,
Embrace the splat, join in the dance.
For every glob that drips and stains,
Is simply joy, no room for pains!

Thorned Elegance

In gardens rich, a throne it claims,
With lacy leaves and prickly aims.
A pretty piece, yet watch your hand,
It's all fun 'til you understand!

With luscious red, it's quite the spark,
But deep inside, it's kind of dark.
One bite will leave your chin aglow,
As sticky juice starts to flow.

So gather friends and take a shot,
At every seed you love or not.
With thorny laughs and jelly smiles,
This fruity curse goes on for miles!

Enigma of the Scarlet Fruit

What hides beneath that crimson hue?
A puzzle wrapped in nature's brew.
With every seed a giggle born,
A jester's crown, or so it's sworn!

It rolls about, a playful sprite,
In every bite, a chuckle bright.
So grab a spoon and dig right in,
But beware the chaos that may win!

Though glossy red may call you near,
Expect the dribble, share the cheer.
For secrets hidden, oh so sneaky,
Make every munch a tad more cheeky!

In the Heart of Rubies

In the heart of rubies, fun awaits,
A splash of laughter on our plates.
Each juicy gem, a burst of glee,
With ruby seeds that yell, "Yippee!"

With every crunch, a silly face,
As juice goes flying in the race.
The more we eat, the more we play,
The fruit of fun, hip-hip-hooray!

So let us dance, let worry cease,
In every bite, a touch of peace.
With smiles wide and joy in sight,
This fruity world feels oh so right!

Crimson Jewels in Autumn's Bounty

In autumn's chill, the fruits do grin,
Their vibrant hues invite us in.
With sticky hands and laughter loud,
We feast like kings beneath the cloud.

Each burst reveals a juicy treat,
We laugh and dance with sticky feet.
The juice runs down like summer rain,
Who knew joy could come with such a stain?

With friends around and skins all red,
We share the tales of what we said.
The treasures found in nature's hand,
Are best enjoyed with laughter's band.

So here's to fruits in autumn's light,
With goofy smiles, we share the bite.
In every seed, a giggle's found,
Let's celebrate this joy unbound!

Whispered Echoes of Forgotten Gardens

In secret gardens, laughter blooms,
Among the weeds, the fun resumes.
With hidden treasures tucked away,
We plot and scheme the perfect play.

"Is this a fruit or alien spawn?"
We poke and prod from dusk till dawn.
With each surprise, a burst of cheer,
We giggle close, no need for fear.

The sun sets low, the shadows sway,
As we indulge in fruit ballet.
With laughter high, we steal a bite,
In whispers shared, the world feels right.

Forgotten fruits, we have our fun,
With silly games till day is done.
In secret spots, our voices blend,
As echoes of joy, we recommend!

Seeds of Desire Beneath the Skin

Beneath the skin, secrets hide strong,
With every bite, we hum a song.
The seeds of whimsy dance and twirl,
In juicy bites, we laugh and swirl.

A squishy mess, we make it grand,
With hands all sticky as we planned.
"Did you get one that tastes like cheese?"
We joke and snicker, such a tease!

Juicy treasures drip and splash,
As we engage in food's wild clash.
With humor high, we make a mess,
In fruit-filled fun—what could be less?

With seeds of desire just within,
Each laugh a victory, where we win.
So bring me more, my fruity knight,
Let's munch until we're full tonight!

A Tapestry of Temptation

In a garden of mischief, we conspire,
With fruits galore, our hearts retire.
Each juicy bite a tantalizing tease,
With sticky fingers, we do as we please.

"Do you think this color will stain my face?"
With giggles shared, we quicken our pace.
A tapestry woven with laughter, bright,
Our fruity feasts feel just so right!

In laughter's embrace, we chuckle and cheer,
The antics continue, the end is not near.
In fruity mischief, we find our place,
Where giggles echo—just look at our grace!

Temptation's bounty, sweet and bold,
In fruity tales, young and old.
So raise your glasses, here's a toast,
To silly times, we love the most!

Secrets Wrapped in Leaves

In a garden where whispers play,
Fruits don cloaks, bright and gay.
Look twice at what hangs in sight,
You might find a berry's delight.

Oh, the peeking and the pry,
Nibbled edges, oh my, oh my!
Each little gem, a riddle to tease,
Nature's jest, if you please!

Beneath those leaves, a party awaits,
Tiny critters on dinner plates.
One sly bird, with a mischievous grin,
Dares to dive in; oh, where to begin?

Curly vines dance in the breeze,
As fruit unfolds secrets with ease.
Laughter echoes in the air,
Come and join, if you dare!

An Ode to the Unseen

In shadows deep, a treasure hides,
With secrets tangled, like floppy rides.
A twisting trunk, a giggle might sound,
As you discover what's lurking around.

A curious taste, sweet yet spry,
What do you mean, did that fruit just sigh?
With each bite, a joke is spun,
Who knew fruit could be so much fun?

This riddle dangles from a tree,
Winking at you; can you see?
Just when you think you've cracked the code,
It plays a prank, on this sweet road.

So munch and crunch, unleash the thrill,
In this orchard, there's always a chill.
With giggles fresh and laughter obscene,
Join us for a slice of the unseen!

Elusive Splendor Beneath

Beneath the foliage, colors collide,
Nature's canvas, a wild ride.
Try to guess what's hiding there,
Is that a secret—or a bear?

Each wrinkled skin, a cheeky tease,
What's inside? A tickling breeze!
Dive into flavors, a carnival round,
With juicy jewels that abound.

Step lightly now, don't make a fuss,
Nature's giggles are quite the plus.
The treasures here, mysteries unfurl,
Savor the wonders, give them a twirl!

So lift your gaze and take your bite,
In this fruit haven, the world feels right.
With secrets wrapped in blushing hues,
Let each explorer find their muse!

The Heartbeat of a Scarlet Sphere

Oh, round and plump, a cherry on a spree,
What swirls inside? A mystery, you see!
With every squeeze, the fruit starts to grin,
Ready to share its juicy whim.

Dressed in red, a festive delight,
Whispering tales beneath the moonlight.
Open it up, don't be shy,
A wild explosion! It's fruit pie in the sky!

With laughter hidden in every seed,
This riotous orb is what we need.
Each heartbeat thumps with zest and cheer,
Join the fun, let's all volunteer!

So grab a spoon, let's dig right in,
Let's make a mess, let the games begin!
Beneath the skin, a secret play,
The heartbeat awaits, come what may!

Clandestine Harvest

In the orchard when no one can see,
Fruits giggle and sway with glee.
They hide their jewels beneath a skin,
Whispering tales of where they've been.

Red beads within, a treasure trove,
A delicacy that makes one rove.
But beware the burst, oh what a mess,
Sticky fingers are part of the jest.

Each seed a story, a tiny laugh,
As juice dribbles down, oh what a path!
Rumors swirl of the taste they hide,
In fruity games, they take great pride.

So when you munch on the crimson treat,
Know it's plotting some mischief, oh so sweet!

Chambers of Sweet Blood

Inside a fruit with a ruby glow,
Lies a party that nobody knows.
Tiny seeds in their fancy dress,
Dance around, no need to impress.

They chatter and chuckle, a lively crowd,
Hiding from folks, feeling quite proud.
One bold seed yells, 'Let's make a mess!'
Splat! The juice flies, it couldn't care less!

Tasting a fruit is quite the quest,
With laughter and juice, it beats all the rest.
But mind the dribble that runs down your chin,
It's part of the fun, let the feast begin!

So join in the revel, don't be shy,
With chambers of joy, oh my oh my!

Hidden Lore in Granate

Elusive truths in every bite,
Secrets hidden, oh what a sight!
Crimson globes with much to share,
Tickle your tongue with tales so rare.

'What's it like in the land of juice?'
One asks the other, 'Have you let it loose?'
They spill the beans on sweet delight,
And visitors leave with smiles so bright.

As you pop one and hear it crack,
You'll laugh aloud, no holding back.
For inside each bite is a bounty of cheer,
A party in fruit, let's raise a beer!

So nibble with glee, let the legends unfold,
In this playful realm where joys are gold!

Echoes of Nature's Riddle

In a world of green, where colors clash,
Bursts of red cause a merry splash.
Ticklish seeds with a cheeky grin,
Whisper sweet secrets of what's within.

Giggles echo as they collide,
Juicy skirmishes they cannot hide.
One brave seed shouts, 'Let's spill the fun!'
Drippy poems under the sun!

Nature's riddle in this playful tease,
With every bite, it aims to please.
So dive right in, without a care,
In this fruity fiasco, laughter's everywhere!

Embrace the chaos, relish the goop,
In echoes of nature, join the troop!

The Twisted Root of Truth

In the garden, roots do dance,
Tickling soil, they plot their prance.
What grows below is a playful lie,
Sprouting laughs as they reach for the sky.

Beneath the earth, the whispers flow,
Riddles exchanged in a dirt-filled show.
They twist and turn, a prankster's feat,
Confusing the gardener, oh what a treat!

Gnarled and bold with a cheeky grin,
They'll trick you into thinking they win.
But laughter erupts, as they come apart,
For roots have a way to soften the heart.

So next time you dig in the ground,
Remember the giggles that echo around.
A garden of jest, where truth is a game,
And all who wander will feel the same.

Tales of the One Who Tastes

There once was a chap who loved to munch,
On fruits of odd colors, often with a crunch.
He bit into one, oh what a surprise!
A flavor explosion that lit up his eyes.

With seeds that popped like little balloons,
He laughed and giggled, singing with tunes.
Each taste was a riddle, each bite a delight,
As crimson juice splattered, oh what a sight!

His friends gathered round, curious to see,
What shenanigans followed a bite from the spree.
They dared to indulge, with a chuckle and cheer,
But oh, that sweet tang led them to fear!

For sticky fingers and laughter galore,
Made them all sticky from ceiling to floor.
Yet in the mess, they found pure glee,
Tales of good times, as sweet as can be.

Paths of Crimson Juice

Down the lane of sweet delight,
Paths of crimson bring pure delight.
Step carefully now, it's a slippery way,
With juice on the rocks that dares you to play.

Each footstep mines a burst of fun,
A stumble leads to giggles, that's how it's done!
Skidding and sliding, the laughter ensues,
Who knew a fruit could ignite such blues?

Adventures await with each vibrant splatter,
Every drop leaves a story, which makes hearts chatter.
So grab on tight and embrace the slide,
For life's a journey, with joy as your guide!

When the sun sets low and the stars gleam bright,
Paths of crimson shine with wonderful light.
For every misstep, in foolish jest,
Brings all together, and that's for the best.

Shadows Among the Leaves

In the garden, shadows play,
Among the leaves, they twirl and sway.
Peeking through with a quirky prance,
Who's hiding there? Come join the dance!

A cheeky breeze whispers secrets near,
As silly insects buzz with cheer.
They gossip 'bout fruits with vibrant skins,
Laughing at kin with delicious sins.

Under green canopies, funny tales spin,
Of berries and melons, where does one begin?
With humor tucked under the boughs overhead,
Every nibble shared fills dreams with dread!

So take a seat, let giggles bloom,
In the shadows where laughter finds room.
For the garden's a stage, with a whimsical cast,
Where secrets are sweet and the fun's unsurpassed.

Nectar of Enigmatic Love

In a garden where juiciness plays,
A fruit with a laugh in the sun's rays.
It wiggles and giggles, ripe on the vine,
Whispering secrets, oh, how divine!

With each little seed, a tale to unfold,
Of crushes and quirks, both timid and bold.
Sipping its nectar, we jest and we tease,
Love's sticky sweetness puts everyone at ease.

Bright red and sassy, it leaps from your hand,
A food fight erupts, isn't life grand?
With splatters of juice like a painter's grand art,
Its juicy delights will tickle your heart.

So grab a spoonful, don't mind the mess,
A dance of the flavors, oh what a fest!
For every dark seed holds laughter inside,
In this fruity affair, let joy be our guide.

Colors of the Forbidden Garden

In shadows of vines where whispers collide,
A fruit wears a gown of scandal and pride.
With pink polka dots and a mischievous grin,
It chuckles, inviting us all to dive in.

Oh, striking and bold, let's break the old rules,
Surrounded by legends, giggling like fools.
Each slice tells a story of mischief and cheer,
In the garden of secrets, come grab your leer.

With colors so naughty, they dance to the beat,
We prance with our spoons, let's feast on this treat!
As laughter erupts and our worries all fade,
Who knew such a beauty could throw such a parade?

So splash on the joy from the tips of our toes,
Beneath the bright blooms, the hilarity grows.
In this garden of colors, let's cherish the spree,
With fruit on our faces, we're wild and free!

Singing Seeds of Fate

Tucked inside a treasure, so small and so round,
Seeds sing in harmony, a whimsical sound.
They giggle and wiggle, a chorus of fun,
Mysteries beckoning under the sun.

Pop one and chuckle, they whisper a tale,
Of love gone awry and a comical fail.
Each burst of flavor, a riddle, a rhyme,
Life's silly moments caught in the prime.

A game with our friends, who can pop the best?
With laughter unloosened, we're put to the test.
Squeezing those fruits like a stress ball of joy,
Unlimited laughter, oh girl and boy!

As echoes of giggles cascade through the air,
Seeds sowing mischief, a grand, goofy affair.
In a world full of fun, under sun's radiant light,
Let seeds guide our dance into the night.

Celestial Containers of Delight

Oh, starry fruit with your shiny facade,
Your laughter-filled chambers have us all awed.
With each little gleam sparkling bright on the shelf,
We crack them open, delighting ourselves.

They're like tiny buddies, with secrets to share,
Each bite a surprise, a whimsical dare.
A dose of pure joy wrapped in soft skin,
Inviting us in for a good, silly grin.

With laughter in heaps and mischief galore,
We toss back the seeds, wanting more and more.
Showering fun like confetti on cake,
Celebrating the moments we joyfully make.

So here's to the delights, our cosmic affair,
With fruity concoctions, let's dance in the air!
In celestial realms where happiness we find,
Containers of giggles, forever entwined.

Nostalgia in Every Seed

Once upon a fruit with a sheen,
Lurking memories bright and green.
Each seed a tale, a laugh, a sigh,
Squeezing juice from the moments gone by.

Grandma's whispers, sweet and bold,
Tales of summers, laughter untold.
I chuckle at each vibrant seam,
Every burst a childhood dream.

Red ruby jewels in a burst of cheer,
Creating mess, we'd have no fear.
Sticky fingers, laughter would glisten,
In every split, the past would listen.

A fruit of joy with its playful hue,
Always reminding of things we knew.
Dancing seeds, oh what a ride,
Nostalgia served, nowhere to hide.

Palate of Hidden Dreams

In a garden of mischief, colors collide,
A fruit with secrets so brightly portrayed.
Hidden dreams in each tiny treat,
Bold adventures, a sugary feat.

Beneath the skin, a party awaits,
Chaotic flavors that dance on plates.
Like a magician, bursting with flair,
Taste buds chuckle in playful affair.

A splash of tang, a tease of sweet,
Filling your mouth, oh what a feat!
Sipping memories, swirling around,
Whispers of dreams in laughter abound.

What's in the bowl? A riddle or jest?
With each little pop, our hearts are blessed.
A canvas of taste we endlessly scheme,
Palate of joy drenched in a dream.

Voices of the Orchard

In the orchard, chatter fills the air,
A fruit's gossip flows without a care.
Seeds giggling, bursting with sass,
Each color a character, a vibrant class.

The boughs sway with stories they share,
A fruit's twist, a playful affair.
Laughter echoes, rising so high,
Nature's comedy under the sky.

Even the bees join in the fun,
Buzzing their rhymes beneath the sun.
The orchard sings with voices so bright,
Chaque fruit joins the joyful light.

Under the leaves, secrets entwine,
In every whisper, a punchline divine.
Silly tales in this lush domain,
Voices of laughter, a fruit-filled refrain.

Entwined in Scarlet

In a swirl of red, mischief abounds,
Little seeds giggle and twirl all around.
Crimson dreams in every delight,
Creating chaos, oh what a sight!

With each juicy pop comes a laugh,
A playful jest, the fruit's autograph.
Messy faces, sticky with glee,
Entwined in scarlet, happy as can be.

What tangy tales lie under the skin?
Every bite's a riddle, let the fun begin!
Like confetti, flavors burst and fly,
Celebrating moments, oh my oh my!

A moment's pleasure, a fruit's wild jest,
Laughter echoes, nature's zesty fest.
Entwined in crimson, hearts celebrate,
In every bite, we just can't wait!

Fragile Kernels of History

In a fruit so bright and red,
Lie treasures that can't be fed.
Each kernel hides a tale so sweet,
It's history wrapped in a juicy treat.

The farmer chuckles with each bite,
Wondering if he's got it right.
He claims it's magic, folks just laugh,
While pondering if they've found the half.

A swig of juice, a squirt and splat,
The kids run wild, the cat goes flat.
With every pop, confusion reigns,
As laughter bursts amid the stains.

So tread with care near juicy dreams,
Where mirth frolics in vibrant beams.
For in this garden of silly zest,
The kernels whisper, "We're the best!"

The Allure of Amber Waters

Beneath the sun, a shimmer glows,
In waters amber, mischief flows.
With every sip, a giggle springs,
Warning: this nectar does funny things!

The fish all dance, a sight to see,
They laugh at folks who can't agree.
A splash, a snort, a gurgle loud,
Where mischief swims, we're all so proud.

Is it the drink? Or just the sun?
In this belly-laughing run!
With every gulp, we're lost in bliss,
The world turns silly, it's hard to miss.

So raise your cups, let's toast the fun,
For spilled drinks under the golden sun.
In laughter's tide, we slip and slide,
In amber waters, let's all abide!

The Gilded Cloak of Mystery

Wrapped in gold, a cloak so bright,
It hides the secrets, oh so right.
What's underneath—could it be a pie?
Or perhaps a dance with a friendly fly?

The crows convene, they caw and prance,
They swear they've caught a glimpse of chance.
With every flap, a riddle plays,
What's hidden there—a dream or craze?

A swirl of laughter lifts the air,
As hints of mischief spark a dare.
To peek beneath or stay away,
What's in the cloak? Come what may!

So gather round, dear friends, don't flee,
Let's lift the edges, let's all agree.
For in that cloak, the joy unfolds,
Mysteries wrapped in laughter's folds!

Corners of the Orchard

In corners green where laughter grows,
The orchard hums, the mischief flows.
From trees that teeter, ripe with glee,
The whispers say, "Come climb with me!"

The squirrels are plotting, tails a-twitch,
While apples form a splendid niche.
Friends gather 'round to share a laugh,
As nature scribbles its silly path.

A leap, a trip, a bounce and roll,
The fruit flies high, but so does the soul.
With every toss, the giggles soar,
Harvesting joy—who could ask for more?

So wander through this playful spree,
Where every fruit holds laughter's key.
In the orchard's corners, come and play,
For joy and giggles are here to stay!

Sweet Bitters of Hidden Truths

In a garden, ripe and round,
Lies a fruit that spins around.
Juicy tales in every bite,
Sweet confessions take to flight.

Gossip drips from every seed,
Whispers bloom where fun may lead.
The crunch of secrets loud and clear,
Makes you laugh till you shed a tear.

Bright red skins with smiles so sly,
What's inside? Oh, come and try!
Sugar-coated, bold and frail,
These hidden truths just love to sail.

So pluck one fresh, don't be absurd,
For laughter's found in every word.
In bites of joy, we'll find our way,
Brightly dancing through the day.

The Allure of Forbidden Harvest

In orchards where the wild winds blow,
A fruit so bright, it steals the show.
Under skirts of leaves it sighs,
Tempting tongues with quirky lies.

"Just one bite!" the tree does tease,
With sweet whispers on the breeze.
Expected joy or sour surprise?
A chuckle forms beneath the guise.

Gather 'round, all ye who dare,
To taste the jest, find laughter rare.
Unraveling tales in juicy floods,
Where mystery meets the cackling buds.

So take a chance, don't miss the fun,
For life's a game that's never done.
In every fruit, a jest concealed,
In every laugh, a truth revealed.

Gardens Where Shadows Bloom

In gardens where all secrets play,
Shadows dance, and children sway.
Beneath the leaves, a riddle grows,
With hints of laughter tucked in rows.

Crimson globes with silly grins,
Hiding laughter where it begins.
Roots of humor twist and twine,
In vine-wrapped jokes, we all entwine.

Take heed, dear friend, do not despair,
For buried jokes are found somewhere.
When shadows bloom, do look around,
The sweetest truths are often found.

In the playful hues of dusk and dawn,
Join the harvest, let joy spawn.
So pluck those gems, for giggles reign,
In the gardens where we dance in rain.

Crimson Threads of Fate

In fields where fate ties knots so tight,
Fruity mischief takes to flight.
Threads of laughter weave and spin,
Beneath the blush of rosy skin.

Crimson orbs serve smiles untold,
While cheeky whispers tease the bold.
A tangled tale within each bite,
With every crunch, a jest ignites.

Secrets burst, a tasty spree,
A giggle here, a snort with glee.
Fate is funny, who would have guessed?
In these fruits, we're truly blessed.

So gather 'round, let's take a chance,
Life's absurd with each ripe dance.
In the threads of laughter, we'll bask tonight,
With every crumb, our hearts alight.

The Weight of Sweetness

With seeds like jewels, a quirky prize,
Each bite a burst, a fruit that lies.
Squeezed juice drips down my chin,
Now sticky fingers, let the fun begin.

Hiding in pockets, the seeds play tricks,
A fruity riddle, oh what a mix.
They promise joy, yet stain my shirt,
A sweet little devil, this cheeky flirt.

In markets loud, they catch my eye,
A red parade that makes me sigh.
I thought a snack, but oh it's true,
I've smuggled home a mini zoo!

Nibbles and giggles, a juicy quest,
In each bite hides a zany jest.
It's fun to share, but watch your face,
This fruit brings joy, but also a race.

Heart of the Earth's Enigma

Beneath the skin, a riddle rests,
With vibrant colors and funny quests.
Each segment hides a world inside,
A little treasure, oh what a ride!

Asking friends to take a bite,
They squirm and laugh, it's quite the sight.
With juice that squirts like silly glee,
It's a game of "not here, not me!"

Crimson balls dancing in a bowl,
I ponder how they play their role.
Like matchmakers of taste and fun,
Creating chaos when I'm done.

Peeling back layers, what's in store?
A slapstick story, seeds galore!
With every nibble, a giggle grows,
What other mischief this fruit knows?

Aroma of Long-Lost Memories

Whiffs of sweetness drift in the air,
Old tales of laughter, without a care.
Each bite collides with flavors past,
In a comedy of tastes, unsurpassed.

Once at the table, a family feast,\nJokes fly around, the laughter increased.
Red juices splatter, like slips and falls,
We cherish the giggles that echo through halls.

Stories unfold, conspiracies brewed,
With each pomegranate, we're back in the mood.
Uncle's wild tales, and Grandma's pie,
The fruit retains all the laughs gone by.

In every crunch, the past takes flight,
Memories sparkling, outrageous delight.
Like a clown with fruit, it steals the show,
In this sweet aroma, we continue to grow.

Cradle of the Scarlet Heart

Nestled in shadows, a vibrant gem,
A fruity joke, a silly whim!
With every seed, a surprise awaits,
Bursting with laughs as it levitates.

In pinkish hued, the mischief reigns,
A dancing fruit with tiny chains.
Open the skin, and there's delight,
A ruby party springs to life tonight.

Watch out, dear friends, for the juice is sly,
It spills and splatters, oh me, oh my!
A sticky situation, but all in good fun,
In this wild ruckus, no one's outdone.

So here we gather with hearts full of joy,
Playing with fruit, every girl, every boy.
In this cradle of laughter, oh what a start,
These juicy antics dance from the heart!

Seeds of Ancient Tales

In the garden of myths, they await,
Little seeds whisper at heaven's gate.
With a giggle, they plot, they're sly,
Prepare for a party, oh me, oh my!

Each round one claims, 'I'm the best!'
While another tries to outdo the rest.
Red jewels gleaming, on branches they sway,
Who knew such trouble would come from play!

The old tales tell of gods with flair,
But these seeds just dance without a care.
"Pick me! Pick me!" they all shout loud,
Creating mischief, as seeds in a crowd.

With laughter sprinkled on every beat,
They burst with cheer, tiny and sweet.
In every bite, a joke or two,
Seeds of fun, always something new!

The Forbidden Fruit's Song

Oh, that fruit that's oh-so-neat,
With secrets covered, isn't it sweet?
A sly grin from that shiny skin,
What lies inside, let the games begin!

The squirrels plot, with crafty schemes,
To snatch the fruit as it gleams.
"Oh dear, what's that?!" a bird squawks loud,
As they dive in, a flurry, a crowd!

A treasure hunt, it's quite the sight,
With every nibble sparking delight.
Taste a seed, it's worth a dare,
For laughter echoes everywhere!

So sing with me of this fruity escapade,
With giggles and tales that won't ever fade.
Each crunch holds a story, oh what fun,
In this wacky world, under the sun!

Cursed with Sweetness

In a land where sweetness ruled the day,
A fruit emerged in a quirky way.
"I'm cursed!" it said with a twinkling pout,
But everyone knew what that fuss was about.

With juicy bites and seeds that tease,
"Just take one more!" it cries with ease.
But as you munch, beware the trap,
For laughter erupts in a happy clap!

Each taste unveils a silly jest,
A fruit that knows how to jest the best.
While ancient foes come to settle a score,
This fruity trickster just begs for more!

So here we are, with laughter and glee,
This sweet little fruit loves to party free.
Join the fun, don't let it pass,
For sweetness here is a real kick-ass!

Red Veins Beneath Skin

Beneath the surface, colors collide,
In red veins hidden, they try to hide.
A wink from a seed, as bright as can be,
Says, "Try me out, come laugh with me!"

With every slice, a drama swells,
Secrets and laughter, like ringing bells.
"Oh, that's a shock!" the tastebuds sing,
When sweetness comes bursting, it's quite the fling!

Mysteries swirl like candy clouds,
With seeds that giggle in playful crowds.
They jump and dance, oh what a sight,
With every crunch, the world feels right!

In this merry dance, let laughter reign,
With silly puns til we're nearly slain.
The magic awaits in those red veins,
So grab a slice and enjoy the gains!

Hidden Stories in Each Segment

In a bright and cheerful orchard,
Little seeds play peek-a-boo.
They giggle behind their red coats,
Whispering tales just for you.

Juicy orbs with a wrinkled grin,
Each slice a riddle wrapped tight.
What happens in the juicy spin,
Remains a bold, delicious sight.

With a crunch and a pop, they burst,
Like confetti on a sunny day.
Their laughter surely quench the thirst,
Of all who stop and wish to play.

Underneath that ruby shell,
Lie tales of sweet and sour fun.
So bite and taste, it's hard to tell,
Which story shines like a hot sun.

A Bounty of Passionate Intrigues

In a world where fruit wears drama,
A rebel seed takes center stage.
With a flair for grand ol' glamor,
It flips the script with every page.

Dancing seeds with wild ambition,
Spin tales of love, life, and cheer.
In every bite, there's a mission,
Behind the juice lies laughter here.

"Why so serious?" a seed will ask,
As they waltz around in delight.
Life's too short for a fussy mask,
Join the party and feel the bite!

So gather 'round, dear snackers bright,
Discover their wild escapades.
Each chunk, a bite of sheer delight,
A bounty deep in fruity parades.

Threads of Color in a Woven World

In a patchwork quilt of fruit so bold,
Each piece a story wrapped in hue.
Crimson threads and secrets told,
Where mischief stars in each view.

Little seeds swing in a juicy rope,
Bouncing to rhythms of laughter.
Though they hope for a chance to elope,
With their buddies in juicy ever after.

A tapestry of tasty pranks,
As they tumble and roll around.
From green to gold, in fruity ranks,
Each segment plays the jester's sound.

Catch the smiles, bright and wise,
In every bite, a laugh to unfurl.
With colors that could mesmerize,
A woven world of juiciness twirls.

The Sorrow of Edible Promises

They make a promise, round and sweet,
To be a snack you can't resist.
Yet underneath this tasty treat,
Lurks a tale of fruit-filled mist.

With crunchy shells and seeds that tease,
They play hide-and-seek with a grin.
Pledging joy, but oh, what a freeze,
When you realize where they've been.

They whisper secrets on a whim,
Of laughter shared in the sun.
Yet in the end, it's a fruity hymn,
As you munch them down one by one.

So savor their quirks and joys,
Each edible promise made in jest.
Though bittersweet with giggling ploys,
These funny gems are simply the best.

www.ingramcontent.com/pod-product-compliance
Lightning Source LLC
Chambersburg PA
CBHW060134230426
43661CB00003B/419